BIGFOOT

Big Foot a name of a cryptic that many have seen. People all over the world have seen this creature. They have even wondered if "IS it really a man"? That is still being proven. Some say that a big foot is an ape. Yet others say it is a man. Some even will say that it is both. But no on really knows what exactly a big foot is. I have been interested in the creature for a while now. I am not an expert on it. I am very interested in it. I love Cryptic creatures and big foot is one of them that I want to go more in depth.

So if we look online and ask "What is a big foot"? We find the many different answers. One is (also known as Sasquatch) is the name given to a mythological simian, ape, or hominid-like creature that is said to inhabit forests, mainly in the Pacific Northwest. In North American folklore, Bigfoot is usually described as a large, hairy, bipedal humanoid. Or a large, hairy, apelike creature resembling a yeti, supposedly found in northwestern America. Yet really we ar not 100% what it is. We do know that a big foot has hair and tall. We know that some features may look like an ape.

So maybe we should look into this creature more. I have gathered different information on this creature from many different sites online and books. I decided to write this book to let others know what information is out there. People should know what is out there. They have the right know that creatures are all around us. There are animals or creatures that are not documented ar have not been seen. Cryptic creatures are these animals. This book is about the famous BIG FOOT. It is made to give others a better understanding about them. Now one thing to know is Big Foot is to be taken as dangerous. No one should walk up to one and expect it to be friendly. No way is that smart.

One question is who created the name Big Foot? (1)

n looking for this information I came across an article. The Man Who Created Bigfoot By: Leah ottile. Leah had written about Bob Gimlin. I want to share that article with you.

or weeks in the fall of 1967 the cowboys rode from sunrise to sunset in search of the creature o one had ever captured on film. Two rodeo men from Washington's apple country, they'd aveled to Northern California's thick forest. They'd read headlines of unidentifiable footprints. he smaller cowboy was driven by a long obsession with the mythic beast known as Bigfoot; the ther liked to see things for himself.

ne late October afternoon near Bluff Creek, the men trundled on horseback, half a day's ride om the nearest signs of civilization. The sun shone bright, lighting the leaves all around them in grand finale of orange and red and yellow. Roger Patterson rode in front, pausing his quarter orse to point his lens toward the leaves, the film chattering inside his rented 16mm Cine Kodak amera. When he finished, he tucked the camera into his saddlebag, leaving the leather flap pen.

Bob Gimlin brought up the rear. He rode a pony, leading a packhorse loaded with supplies behind him. Patterson navigated around a bend where a large tree had fallen and jammed up the nearby creek—its root system upturned and exposed, like blind fingers reaching for an anchor.

The horses saw it first. Patterson's reared, kicking and protesting, then Gimlin's. Less than 100 feet away, the men saw why: a hulking gorilla-like figure covered in dark hair hurried on two legs along the creekbed. Its sloped head and torso were pushed forward, its upper back hunched, thigh muscles rippling, long arms swinging, breasts exposed.

Patterson scrambled off his spooked animal, holding its reins just long enough to reach inside his saddlebag for the camera. Gimlin, a cowboy famous through the Yakima Valley for taming wild colts and running in breakneck "suicide races" (in which riders careen down steep slopes), dropped the packhorse's rope and gripped the reins of his frightened pony to steady it.

Patterson scrambled across the uneven ground, waving the camera in one hand, the film blurry as he ran. He stopped to crouch and steady himself, then trained the lens on the strange figure, the camera shaking from his breathing. "Bob! Cover me!" he yelled over his shoulder to Gimlin, who rode toward the creek, dismounting his pony and drawing his rifle.

The picture steadied as the creature, mid-stride, turned to look over its right shoulder—just a glance—before it disappeared into the forest. A skunky, rank odor hung heavy in the air. The whole affair was over in less than a minute.

he final 59.5-second film, which the men would airmail back home to be developed, would

oon become the world-famous Patterson-Gimlin film—arguably one of the most scrutinized

ieces of video footage ever made. It is the cryptozoological equivalent to the Kennedy

ssassination's Zapruder film. The film met immediate criticisms accusing Patterson and Gimlin

f being master pranksters who simply filmed a man in an ape suit and laid fake footprints in the

ud.

he film tore Patterson's and Gimlin's friendship apart. Patterson partnered with his brother-in-

w, Al DeAtley, to take the film on a national tour as a way to raise funds for a full-fledged

xpedition back at Bluff Creek. The three took equal shares in the film, but soon Gimlin felt

dged out, and sold his share of the rights for less than $10 to another Bigfoot researcher.

fter five years estranged, Patterson and Gimlin made amends in 1972 as Patterson lay on his

eathbed, dying of cancer at age 38. Patterson apologized for ousting Gimlin, pleading with him that when he recovered that they would go back to California and catch Bigfoot. He died the next day.

More than 40 years later, the film has never been conclusively debunked. It has withstood scrutiny from scientists, forensic analysts, Hollywood special effects experts, and costume designers. No one can quite explain it—except those who believe in folklore. In that time, Bigfoot has evolved into a full-fledged American myth, propagated by a national congregation of believers who regard Gimlin as a kind of prophet.

"Meeting Bob Gimlin, to a Bigfooter, is like meeting the President of the United States to an American," says Cindy Rose Caddell, a researcher and author. "Or what meeting the Pope is to a Catholic."

The 84-year-old cowboy wore a black cattleman's hat and sunglasses, an off-white coat with "Bob" embroidered in blue thread at the chest. His boots stated their intentions across the tile entryway of a roadside diner in Union Gap, in central Washington, pausing as he held the door for an elderly woman in a pink jacket.

"Come on in, young lady," he said, his baritone voice all campfire smoke and truck engines. Bob Gimlin wears big hats and big belt buckles and drives a big pickup. He talks slow with a heavy drawl and seems to find a way to turn almost any conversation toward horses.

In a booth with vinyl seats, Gimlin ordered coffee and dumped in two creams, and told the waitress he wouldn't be eating. For the next six hours, he told his story: who he was before he saw Bigfoot, who he became after, and why he stayed quiet for four decades after the film's debut.

efore he had ever heard of Bigfoot, Gimlin had led the life of a man who feared nothing, who

rived on dares and several times cheated death. The first time was at age seven when his

pendix burst. He missed a year of school as he recovered in the Ozark mountains cabin in

issouri where he was born.

1940, the promise of sprawling green ranchlands and orchards set against the towering

ascades pulled his farmer father and part-Apache mother westward. In Washington, Gimlin

ped wild horses with native boys on the nearby Yakima Reservation, crawling onto their backs

d hanging on for dear life. "I was ready to ride," he says. "Even at a very young age I wanted

ride anything that bucked, jumped, moved, run, or whatever." He became a natural rodeo man:

ick to bounce back, never letting a cast or a sling keep him from a horse. He raced caravans

d chariots through mountain passes, hurtled down cliffsides. He gained a reputation as a

redevil (though he declined Evel Knievel's offer to join him in for-profit "daredevilin'").

age 18, Gimlin joined the Army reserves; later he enlisted in the Navy. After two tours in the

orean War, he and three other sailors were in a car accident that left one dead when the driver

nashed into a power pole. His head slammed into the dash and the motor of the car pinned his

dy in the vehicle. "I lost half my face," he says. Gimlin underwent several plastic surgeries to

pair his nose. He spent two years recovering in a hospital in California. Once he received his

scharge papers, Gimlin headed back home to Yakima.

fe, for Gimlin, continued on a normal course: he married, had children, divorced, then married

he sassiest thing I'd ever met"—his wife of 52 years, Judy. In 1967, Gimlin, then 35, was

raping together a living driving trucks, roofing, and riding and taming horses. There was nothing significant about the day he pulled into a Union Gap service station and ran into his old rodeo pal, Roger Patterson.

Patterson was recovering from a bout with cancer. As they spoke, Patterson told Gimlin of his interest in supposed Bigfoot sightings. "He said, 'Let me show you something,'" Gimlin recalls "He went over to the truck and brought out a plaster cast of a big foot." Patterson asked Gimlin he would be interested in searching Mount St. Helens on horseback with him for evidence of a Bigfoot. "I said, 'Roger, I just don't have time.'"

By the late 1960s, Bigfoot had been tromping through Northwestern lore for hundreds of years. Several Native American tribes tell of looming, furry beasts reeking of scorched hair who stole trout from fishermen. In the early 20th century, newspaper articles reporting sightings read like spooky stories to tell around a campfire. In one such report, from 1924, a clan of rock-throwing ape-men ambushed a group of miners on Mt. St. Helens. The place is now called Ape Canyon. (Skeptics said the beasts were just YMCA campers playing a prank.) Ivan Sanderson's 1961 book, Abominable Snowmen: Legend Come to Life, read like the stuff of a B movie.

But there were few opportunities for Patterson to commune with other believers. So he talked to Gimlin: the men formed a bond, riding horses through Washington's backcountry. Patterson continued to regale Gimlin with Bigfoot lore, playing him recorded testimonies of real-life encounters and lending him books on the topic, despite Gimlin's insistence that he did not care. (Patterson self-published a book in 1966, titled Do Abominable Snowmen of America Really Exist?)

Then, in August 1967, Patterson told Gimlin about a logging road construction crew spotting tracks and having their equipment inexplicably disassembled deep in the Six Rivers National orest. He begged Gimlin to drive the two men and their horses to Northern California to search. imlin was skeptical that anything existed, but he was intrigued, and he wasn't the sort of man) turn away from a good adventure. "I wanted to see these footprints that these people talked bout," he says.

he film the men produced gave the murky myth shape: suddenly, Bigfoot was manifested in esh and blood. It had a loping gait and, with the twist of its torso, it looked over its shoulder efore disappearing again into the wilderness. It even had a name: Patty.

atty, arguably, created the Bigfoot industry. Today, the apelike figure—frozen in its signature rn—adorns car air fresheners and infant onesies that read, "Believe." It looks back from coffee ips, Christmas ornaments, guitar picks, and Band Aids. There's a Patty-shaped Chia Pet. igfoot even has a home on reality TV: Animal Planet launched Finding Bigfoot in 2011, arring Washington's Bigfoot Field Researchers Organization (BFRO). BFRO members lead uided backwoods expeditions—with a price tag of up to $500—throughout the U.S. where articipants scour the forests for a look at the fabled beast.

ut looking back on the trip today, Gimlin wishes he'd said no. That he'd turned away from atterson that day at the service station and never looked back.

hat trip to California changed him.

t ruined me."

y 1972, Patterson had died. Gimlin alone faced the scourge of detractors that were emerging ound the country—some even confronted he and his wife in their hometown. Yakima was the place where Gimlin had become known for his fearlessness and strength, and suddenly he was a seen as crazy. His word, his handshake—currency around this part of the state—was in doubt.

"My wife was a teller at a savings and loan institution. Of course, she was sitting right there and the public would come in and make smart remarks," Gimlin says. "This went on and on and on until she come home crying. She'd say, 'I'm not tough enough.' A couple times we were going to split up over this."

Some nights, cars would screech by the Gimlins' house. "They'd come driving in my driveway all times of the night and go 'Bob! We want to go out Bigfoot hunting!'" he says. They'd speed away before he could run outside.

The couple felt isolated, and Gimlin found himself for the first time in the predicament that cam to define his life for decades: if he acknowledged that he saw Bigfoot, he was the town loon; if he stayed quiet, people assumed he was lying.

"I can understand why they don't believe in it—because I didn't believe it either," Gimlin recall telling John Green, a prominent Canadian Bigfoot researcher, on a phone call during this period "But I saw one. And I know what I saw. And I know it wasn't a man in a suit. It couldn't have been!"

In 1968, the year after Patterson and Gimlin returned, the Gimlins swore to never speak of Bigfoot again. But the video was out, and Gimlin was—and remains—stuck to the center of the debate, anchored like the sun in a growing solar system with believers and skeptics orbiting around him.

eports of sightings filtered in from all over the Northwest. Bigfoot was traipsing through lush oastal woods and rocky mountainsides in Oregon. Its glowing red eyes peered from the nderstory in Olympic National Forest in Washington. It stalked the Dark Divide, the massive oadless area between Mount St. Helens and Mount Adams. It ran across a road near Vancouver. : left footprints in the snow outside Walla Walla.

elievers cropped up in Texas and Ohio, then as far afield as New York, Georgia, and Florida. In he past 40 years, people have produced supposed Bigfoot hairs, DNA tests, footprints, and piles f scat—not to mention the countless photographs and video clips (most of which have turned ut to be hoaxes)—as scientific evidence of the creature's existence. To many, the notion of belief' is irrelevant among the myriad stories, sightings, and artifacts.

No, I don't believe in Bigfoot," says Jeff Meldrum, an anthropology and anatomy professor at laho State University who is one of the foremost experts on foot morphology in the world. He as 11 years old in 1968 when he watched Patterson-Gimlin's Bigfoot walk across the screen at te Spokane Coliseum in Eastern Washington. Today, he's the keeper of the largest archive of igfoot footprint casts and author of the book Sasquatch: Legend Meets Science. "Belief usually onnotes a position of faith, a conviction held in the absence of evidence," Meldrum says. "I, for ne, am convinced by the evidence I have studied at length."

ynics, however, don't just question the "evidence," they question Patterson's and Gimlin's redibility. In 2004, Greg Long, author of one of the most oft-cited pieces of skepticism about te Patterson-Gimlin Film—a book called The Making of Bigfoot—taunted Gimlin from the nal pages of his book: "Will he ever confess?" Long wrote.

"I'm going to be blunt with you," Long said recently over the phone. "I consider Bob Gimlin a liar. I think he's a con artist."

But Long's arguments seem just as flimsy as believers' proof. His book is filled with circumstantial evidence: a costume maker named Philip Morris in the early 2000s said he sold Patterson the suit but couldn't provide any evidence of the sale; a Yakima man named Bob Hieronimus said he was the one that wore it. Neither claim is backed by concrete proof.

"'They can't exist, therefore they don't exist,'" is the message Meldrum has received from skeptics, he says. "That was the actual retort hurled at me by an anthropology colleague."

With Bigfoot having grown into an industry, Long says there's no reason to believe anyone invested in the debate is telling the truth. "They need it to be real," he says. The people who trul believe and search, he adds, "are driven emotionally, I believe, to find Bigfoot."

In the face of skepticism and mockery, a large community of believers views Gimlin as the original seer: the man who witnessed the unthinkable, who lived to tell the tale, and who has been harassed for what he swore was real. These people congregate at Bigfoot conventions around the world to swap stories, trade evidence-gathering techniques and commune with kinfolk. Together they can be "out" about their beliefs.

Gimlin first appeared at a convention in California in 2003. Through his years of silence, Gimli maintained contact with several prominent Bigfoot aficionados, including Swiss researcher Rene Dahinden and a Russian author named Dmitri Bayonov. After years of urging Gimlin to come to Russia to speak about the film, Bayonov arranged to come to America. With Green's help, the pair convinced Gimlin to attend the Willow Creek International Bigfoot Symposium: an event that promised to bring all the biggest scientific names into one room (including Jane Goodall, a imatologist and Bigfoot believer, who canceled her appearance last minute) in the very same ea where Patterson and Gimlin made their film decades before.

> Gimlin, walking into the conference was like entering a church. "It's not a fairy tale to them. 's serious business," he says. "When I met those people down there, they accepted me with hat you call open arms."

here, Gimlin spoke of Bigfoot for the first time in years. "There wasn't a sound in the room hile I was talking," he says. "I thought, 'I can't really believe this. This is almost like seeing igfoot.' God, I felt like I was 10 feet tall."

hen he finished, the room rose to its feet.

"hey just stood up and applauded and applauded," Gimlin says. "I thought, 'Why have I gone > years through a bunch of ridicule?'"

imlin appears at conventions across the country. He signs shirts and plaster foot casts, tells and tells the story of he and Patterson's encounter. He is no stranger to standing ovations.

"hey want to talk to me, they want to tell me about their experience," he says. "This turned my hole life around."

t home in Central Washington, however, Gimlin is no celebrity. When I visited him this past ring, we took a drive through Wapato, just south of Yakima, to see the house where he grew ', only to find a field of weeds where it once stood. His high school is gone, too. Panaderias d taquerias dot the streets he once knew. As he idled on one street, people on the sidewalk rned to look at the cowboy in his truck, staring at him as if he'd just dropped in from outer ace.

Gimlin's days are typical retired-rancher stuff: he wakes at 5 a.m. every morning on his modest 1,500-square-foot home that sits on two acres in town. He leases land around the Yakima area where he grazes his seven horses. He mows his pastures on a riding mower and tends to his garden of cucumbers and tomatoes. At night he watches UFC fights. He's a member of several local equestrian clubs.

Three days a week, Gimlin drives his black pickup—one with a Bigfoot sticker in a tinted back window and Bigfoot air freshener tucked into a cup holder—into town for physical therapy. In the 1990s, Gimlin was bucked off a horse and told by a doctor he'd never ride again. "I proved could do it," he says. But then, in the early 2000s, he went sailing off another horse. He had his bicep removed from his left arm and nearly lost all ability to use it. He lifts light dumbbells now an attempt to regain some feeling.

Every couple of months, he travels to address another congregation of the faithful. People of every age and shape packed inside a Portland beerhall on a Friday night this past January to see Gimlin speak. He told the story he's told a hundred times before, from the beginning: bumping into Patterson at the service station; the bright fall leaves; the creature glancing over its shoulder the conversation at Patterson's bedside hours before he died.

Afterwards, Gimlin stuck around to take pictures and sign autographs. A boy in a red plaid shirt and a cowboy hat holding a 16mm Cine Kodak camera—like the one used to shoot the Patterson Gimlin film—and a plaster footprint cast approached him for a photo.

A few months later, while doing research for this article, I absentmindedly search "#pattersongimlin" on Instagram. A familiar face pops up on my screen. It's that boy in the cowboy hat from January who got a photo with his hero, Bob Gimlin.

he boy's account is practically devoted to Bigfoot. There are photos from the Portland event, ld pictures of Roger Patterson, shots of book covers adorned with furry beasts and more of giant ot casts on his bedroom carpet.

's just one small example of Gimlin's outsized impact on American lore. The Internet has xposed people to the Patterson's and Gimlin's journey in ways unimaginable to Gimlin, and ontinues to enchant new generations of believers. Whether or not any of the stories are true, igfoot is alive and well. In large part, that's because Gimlin, the non-believer, an unlikely hampion of the myth, helped catch a glimpse of it on film.

1 one post, the boy splits the frame in thirds, filling each with photos of Roger Patterson's ravestone. "We never forget he was our Bigfoot hunter," he writes. A portion of another caption ads: "I met Bob Gimlin…it was a best day ever #bobgimlin."

---

ow everyone will have their own opinion on this whole thing. Some believe that tape was real. thers believe they had someone in a monkey outfit walk across. The whole thing is really up to hatever your mind wants you to believe. Now here is a twist for you to think about. IF that tape as faked, then why are people all over the world seeing the same thing? Sure they may have ifferent various ways of describing it. But how could they all pretty much match up? There is a uestion for people to look at.

ow the next question some people want to know is where did they come from?

ell here is unanswered question. We really do not know for 100% as to where they came from. e can only guess where they are from. So in trying to figure out where they come from one site ctually gives a good idea as to where they think they come from.

BFRO (2) says;

"Bigfoot research" is a term loosely used to describe any efforts to probe or explain the reports and physical evidence associated with bigfoots. Over the years several different theories have been offered. Some of the more common theories are: 1) fear manifestations, 2) misidentifications of bears, 3) paranormal / UFO-related, 4) the Collective-Memory hypothesis, 5) the Bigfoot-Giganto hypothesis.

Bigfoot advocates as well as informed skeptics generally do not believe a hoax is responsible for this phenomenon, primarily because the observations extend so far back in time.

The patterns among eyewitnesses are not demographic, they are geographic -- they are not reported by certain types of people, rather by people who venture into certain areas. This simple pattern suggests an external cause.

No matter what that cause is, it is important to understand, and not just because of the potential behind the most likely explanation.

Bigfoot researchers generally lean toward one explanation: The Bigfoot-Giganto Theory (hypothesis). The subject of Gigantopithecus has attracted an increasing amount of interest anthropologists and primatologitsts over the past few decades. The Bigfoot-Giganto hypothesis uggests that bigfoots are surving relatives of the genus Gigantopithecus. Gigantopithecus (the

atin word for "Giant Ape") was a giant cousin of the orangutan. It was presumed to be extinct.

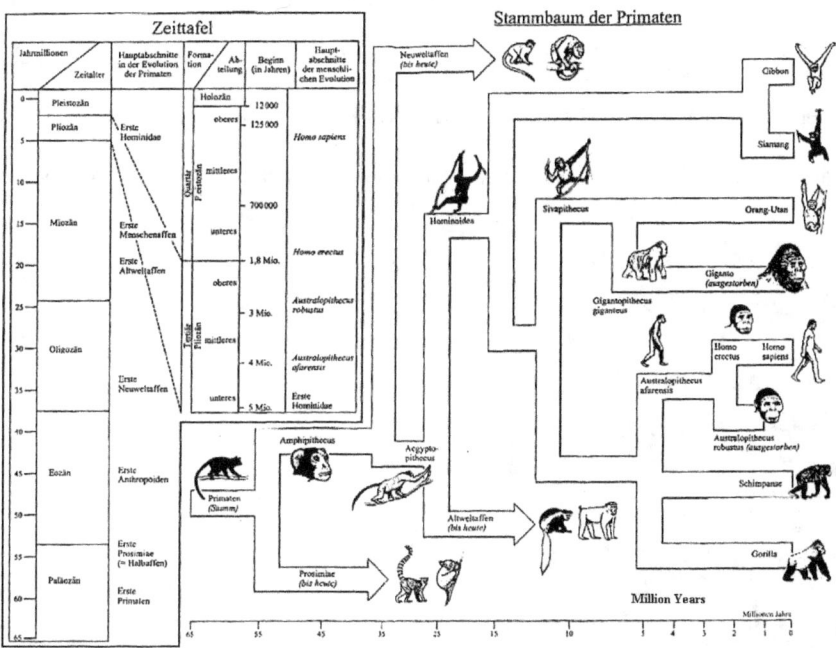

igfoot-Giganto theorists deal with a few issues that affect the potential linkage of modern

igfoot reports to ancient Gigantos. Probably the most crucial question concerns whether

igantos walked upright. There is more than one school of thought among anthrolopogists

egarding this issue. Some physical anthropologists interpret the scant fossilized remains to

idicate an upright walking ape, measuring an impressive nine feet tall, and weighing more than

)00 pounds -- the general description of bigfoot type creatures reported for centuries in North

America and Asia. Even if Giganto posture is uncertain, no one can reasonably dispute the conclusion that Gigantos were the largest primates that ever walked the earth.

Bigfoot-Giganto theorists believe that Gigantos' large brain size (perhaps the largest in the terrestrial animal kingdom) and upright-walking posture facilitated their dispersion across Asia and North America. Thousands of years of adaptation to temperate and mountainous climates, is believed, would have given these large upright walking apes the ability to tolerate cold temperatures, climb through deep snow, and cross high mountain ranges with relative ease.

 The figure to the left is a photo of a life-size Giganto reconstruction based on fossilized remains (click on the photo to see a larger version; the same reconstruction is pictured below with the sculptor showing its size relative to humans). The first photo is from the cover of a book about Gigantopithecus. The translation of the German title is "Why Did Giganto Have to Die?" (The original English version of the book is titled, "Other Origins".)

here is some physical evidence to indicate that Gigantos in Asia were hunted and eaten by omo erectus (ancestors to humans that lived contemporaneously with Gigantos). The ainstream explanation for the apparent disappearance of Gigantos lays blame primarily on this edation by Homo erectus. Bigfoot-Giganto theorists do not accept the idea that a highly mobile nus like Gigantopithecus could have been completely wiped out by Homo erectus. Instead they ok to consistencies in present day bigfoot reports and see the necessary behavioral adaptations nich would have allowed the Giganto line to avoid extinction at the hands of man.

gfoots are typically sighted in or near remote wooded, mountainous, or swampy areas. They e rarely seen far from the cover of trees. If they encounter humans during daylight hours they nd to retreat and vanish into the forest. They seem to be most active when humans are least tive -- late at night. Unlike mountain gorillas, bigfoots are never seen in large groups, and they n't stay in the same place for very long.

ne ellusiveness of these modern mystery animals may stem from their bad experiences with e-humans in Asia.

ne Hypothesis

gfoot Field Researchers Organization Logo

Hypotheses & Research Projects

Ohio Eyewitness Sketches

Ohio Field Recording

Ohio Deer Kills

Powered by Translate

The Bigfoot-Giganto Theory

Background

"Bigfoot research" is a term loosely used to describe any efforts to probe or explain the reports and physical evidence associated with bigfoots. Over the years several different theories have been offered. Some of the more common theories are: 1) fear manifestations, 2) misidentifications of bears, 3) paranormal / UFO-related, 4) the Collective-Memory hypothesis, 5) the Bigfoot-Giganto hypothesis.

Bigfoot advocates as well as informed skeptics generally do not believe a hoax is responsible for this phenomenon, primarily because the observations extend so far back in time.

The patterns among eyewitnesses are not demographic, they are geographic -- they are not reported by certain types of people, rather by people who venture into certain areas. This simpl pattern suggests an external cause.

No matter what that cause is, it is important to understand, and not just because of the potential behind the most likely explanation.

Bigfoot researchers generally lean toward one explanation: The Bigfoot-Giganto Theory (hypothesis). The subject of Gigantopithecus has attracted an increasing amount of interest anthropologists and primatologitsts over the past few decades. The Bigfoot-Giganto hypothesis suggests that bigfoots are surving relatives of the genus Gigantopithecus. Gigantopithecus (the Latin word for "Giant Ape") was a giant cousin of the orangutan. It was presumed to be extinc

Click on the figure to the upper right to see a chart showing the place of Gigantos in primate evolution.

Bigfoot-Giganto theorists deal with a few issues that affect the potential linkage of modern bigfoot reports to ancient Gigantos. Probably the most crucial question concerns whether Gigantos walked upright. There is more than one school of thought among anthrolopogists

garding this issue. Some physical anthropologists interpret the scant fossilized remains to
dicate an upright walking ape, measuring an impressive nine feet tall, and weighing more than
000 pounds -- the general description of bigfoot type creatures reported for centuries in North
merica and Asia. Even if Giganto posture is uncertain, no one can reasonably dispute the
onclusion that Gigantos were the largest primates that ever walked the earth.

igfoot-Giganto theorists believe that Gigantos' large brain size (perhaps the largest in the
rrestrial animal kingdom) and upright-walking posture facilitated their dispersion across Asia
d North America. Thousands of years of adaptation to temperate and mountainous climates, it
believed, would have given these large upright walking apes the ability to tolerate cold
mperatures, climb through deep snow, and cross high mountain ranges with relative ease.

he figure to the left is a photo of a life-size Giganto reconstruction based on fossilized remains
lick on the photo to see a larger version; the same reconstruction is pictured below with the
ulptor showing its size relative to humans). The first photo is from the cover of a book about
igantopithecus. The translation of the German title is "Why Did Giganto Have to Die?" (The
riginal English version of the book is titled, "Other Origins".)

here is some physical evidence to indicate that Gigantos in Asia were hunted and eaten by
omo erectus (ancestors to humans that lived contemporaneously with Gigantos). The
ainstream explanation for the apparent disappearance of Gigantos lays blame primarily on this

predation by Homo erectus. Bigfoot-Giganto theorists do not accept the idea that a highly mobile genus like Gigantopithecus could have been completely wiped out by Homo erectus. Instead the look to consistencies in present day bigfoot reports and see the necessary behavioral adaptations which would have allowed the Giganto line to avoid extinction at the hands of man.

Bigfoots are typically sighted in or near remote wooded, mountainous, or swampy areas. They are rarely seen far from the cover of trees. If they encounter humans during daylight hours they tend to retreat and vanish into the forest. They seem to be most active when humans are least active -- late at night. Unlike mountain gorillas, bigfoots are never seen in large groups, and they don't stay in the same place for very long.

The ellusiveness of these modern mystery animals may stem from their bad experiences with pre-humans in Asia.

The Hypothesis

Over the past 500,000 years hominids gradually emerged from the thickest forests and began to organize into more stationary settlements. Gigantos remained semi-nomadic in the thick forests. Small family groups of Gigantos were widely dispersed in these forests. This dispersal provided more reliable foraging. It also made quick, quiet evasion much easier.

nall Giganto families of 2-4 wandered nomadically through vast forests. The territories were ally remote, but sometimes bordered human settled areas. After thousands of generations they veloped some amazing evasion/defense mechanisms and behaviors, including night vision ilities. They also developed powerful vocal abilities, which allowed them to locate and interact ith others of their kind. They made powerfully loud screams and howls that could be heard for iles in the dead of night. Late hours allowed them to avoid various undesirables: human ingers, overheating, water loss, and the worst insects. The night time vocalizations, and cassional tracks, were usually the only things noted by humans in the area.

Paleoanthro-sculptor Bill Munns
with his Giganto reconstruction
in his Los Angeles backyard.

The most commonly heard argument against the gfoot-Giganto hypothesis is that "we should have found their bones in North America by w..." This argument is, in fact, weak when one considers that very few remains of Gigantos ve ever been found in Asia, where they were much more abundant. Tens of thousands of years Gigantos' accepted existence in Asia would have produced literally millions of Giganto skeletons, yet the volume of collected remains from Asia is so small that the entire collection could fit easily in one suitcase.

Gigantopithecus (Tropical)   Gigantopithecus (Temperate)   6' Tall Human

One flavor of the Bigfoot-Giganto hypothesis suggests that bigfoots might not be direct descendants of the genus Gigantopithecus, but rather some other offshoot of the giant Asian "wood ape" line, perhaps a line for which we have zero fossils remains at the present time. The Giganto line is an important reference point for this alternate explanation for two reasons: 1) the Giganto line illustrates the potential for primates t grow to such 'gigantic' proportions (twice as large as the largest 'known' living primate), and 2 the fact that so few remains of Gigantos have been unearthed and identified makes it more conceivable that there could have been other lines of giant Asian wood apes for which we hav no fossil remains at the present time.

People often assume that bones of a wild animal are present and available long after the anima death. Many people assume that wild animal bones always become fossilized. The fact is bone become fossilized or otherwise preserved only in the rarest of circumstances. Without fossilization or preservation, bones of wild animals will, in time, become completely reabsorb to the biomass. We would literally be climbing over piles of animal bones if they were not naturally recycled. An animal carcass in a dense forest will be reabsorbed relatively quickly through weathering, decay and scavenging by other animals and insects. The odds are very very poor that bones of a rare, elusive, forest dwelling species will be found in some recognizable form by a hiker cruising along a trail.

No research group has ever made an attempt to look for Giganto bones in North America, so no one should be surprised that Giganto remains have never been identified in North America. Ironically, the most vocal skeptics and scientists who rhetorically ask why no bones have been located and identified on this continent are the last people who would ever make an effort to look for them. Some Bigfoot-Giganto theorists speculate that fragmentary remains of Gigantos have been unearthed in North America in the past but were simply disregarded or misidentified.

The second most common argument against the Bigfoot-Giganto hypothesis asks " Why haven't hunters shot one in North America yet ? ..." The reasons are more obvious than most people might realize, and there's enough of them to make a separate article on that topic.

The third most common argument against the Bigfoot-Giganto hypothesis asks " Why aren't there more photos of these modern Gigantos ? ..."

So that is one theory as to where they really come from. There is some that may say they are not from here at all. Really again it is how others see it and what they truly believe. The fact is they are here now. What do they want? That is something that has never been answered. Yet who knows why they are here. All we do know is they are here now. They are huge. They can be dangerous. We also know that they are seen all over. We do know that they a creature we never seen before. So maybe we should look at the anatomy of them. This will hopefully give more an outlook on these mystical creatures.

BFRO (2)

The sasquatch is a large, hairy, bipedal non-human primate that is distributed over the North American continent to varying degrees of concentration. Its massiveness, deviation from human bearing and different gait leave no doubt in the mind of observers that they have seen a creature different from man or known animals.

Skin

Skin color ranges from the deepest black or charcoal to deep brown, "sunburned" reddish brown and gray. Some areas, like the nose, appear at times in a shiny, oily black color. The palms are lighter in color, and the soles of the feet quite light, presumably as a result of thick sole pads composed, as in other primates, of fat and connective tissue. A few albinistic sasquatches have been seen, whose skin color was pink.

Hair

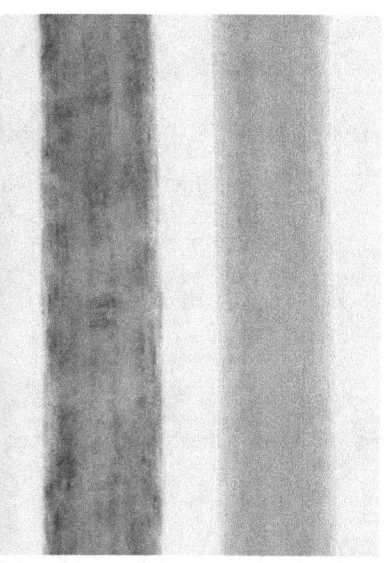

he sasquatch is covered with hair, not fur. Fur has guard hairs and an undercoat, while primate
air consists of one type of hair alone. The sasquatch, being a primate, does not molt its hair, but
 is replaced one hair at a time, hence is not found in wooly batches.

olor of the hair ranges from black or dark (50%), through various shades of reddish-brown and
ray to white. The body can have varicolored patches of hair. Older animals have increasingly
rey hair, though color does not appear to change from childhood to adulthood. Hair is variously
lossy clean and shiny, fluffy, or dirty, matted and unkempt ("angora goat dreadlocks"),
robably a function of native curliness, age, or of recent immersion in water or lack thereof.
emales have been reported to be cleaner than males.

air length ranges from 3" to around 2' (15" longest measured in hand, longer observed in the
ild). There is no taper or color banding other than graying with age. Long hair covers the head
ad, almost invariably, the ears; very short hair on the face; occasional reports of heavy hairiness
 male faces ("mustache" and "beard") vs. no facial hair in females; long hair across the top of

the shoulders (once described as "bouncing like a cape"); long hair on the forearms ("like a spaniel"); different orientations of hair on back; breasts in females hair covered (contrary to a mistaken claim in the literature); long hair on buttocks, sometimes overhanging them; groin with enough hair to obscure genitalia; and long hair on the calves (like "bellbottom pants" in a sasquatch observed standing in snow). The hair stood visibly on end in situations where the sasquatch appeared frightened.

Under the microscope the average diameter of hair is 65 μm (40-90 μm), these values derived from 15 separately collected samples in four States. The cortex has a uniform reddish tinge plus fine pigment granule distribution, whereas the medulla is absent. Intense efforts at DNA analysis of the hair have been uniformly negative, possibly a function of the lacking medulla. Most human hair has a medulla, if only fragmentary, but fine blond hair occasionally looks similar to sasquatch hair. Hence, there is no absolute distinction that can be made. Hair from other forest species, like rodents, carnivores, and ungulates can be differentiated without question.

Odor

About 10-15% of close encounters are connected with an intense, disagreeable stench, comparable to the odor of smegma. Gorillas under conditions of distress exude a gagging, overpowering aroma, the origin of which is the axillary organ, i.e., the armpit with its apocrine sweat glands. The same anatomy probably pertains to the sasquatch.

Many reports refer to uneasiness of man or animals ("being watched") well ahead of any subsequent encounter. A pheromone effect has been suggested, meaning the release of a behavior pattern, "fight or flight", by an airborne molecule. Although this substance might

iginate from the same anatomical location as the odor, the two are not equivalent and should
ot be confused.

ead and Neck

he head, though massive by direct comparison to that of man, has been described as "relatively"
nall for an animal of that size, indicative of a rather small brain. The head develops a sagittal
est in adult males as well as in females, probably bony, which sometimes produces the effect of
person wearing a hooded sweatshirt. Some animals, possibly younger, have a round head.
rain volume is probably close to or slightly above that of the gorilla.

here is a conspicuous brow ridge with a receding forehead, giving the eyes a deep-set look. The
ce is rather flat with prominent cheekbones, a square jaw, and the mouth region is only slightly
otuberant. Deep brown eye color predominates, with a "red" component common (probably a
oodshot sclera). A white sasquatch was reported to have blue eyes. Night reflection from eyes
ries most commonly between red and yellow and is probably dependent on pupillary size
ther than true reflectivity.

he nose is near human in shape, though "pug" or flat, sometimes with forward directed nostrils.
he mouth is often reported to be thin-lipped, with yellowish, square teeth with human
pearance. When larger canines have been seen, they did not project substantially beyond the
ane of the other teeth and would be subject to wear with time. Ears are almost invariably
dden under hair and have been reported to be either rounded or pointed.

uscles from the back of the head flare out to the shoulders to obscure the neck. A result is that,
 in weight lifters, the body is usually turned with the head when a rearward view is desired.

Overall, sasquatches seem to exhibit as much individual diversity in looks as do people, ranging from a typical ape appearance to one described as "an old Indian". The cause may well be the result of the animal not being subject to predation, its young being nurtured and protected into near adulthood, and differences in appearance not being a selective handicap. The same considerations apply to the diversity of coat colors.

Trunk

The trunk is generally carried at a forward angle of about 15° ("hunched over"). This means that the species has not achieved a full upright stance, a difference from human beings, although at times the animals stand up straight. When ultimately a specimen comes to hand, the hip anatomy will be of telling importance to the evolution of an upright stance.

The shoulders are proportionately wider than those of man, measuring about 40% of the height a sasquatch compared to 25-30% in man. Large sasquatches have been described as having four to five foot wide shoulders. They are barrel-chested, with a large respiratory tidal volume, often commented upon when their stertorous breathing has been heard. The Patterson sasquatch (filmed in the famous 1967 movie), a female slightly below the mean height of the population, has a chest circumference of about 60" (a value calculated from available images). This circumference would be about 65" for the average-sized animal and well above 75" for the largest individuals that have been seen.

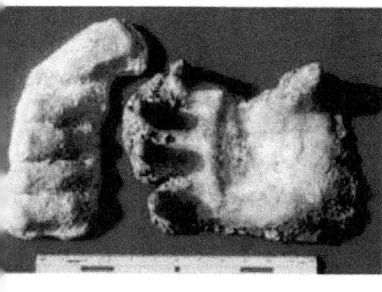 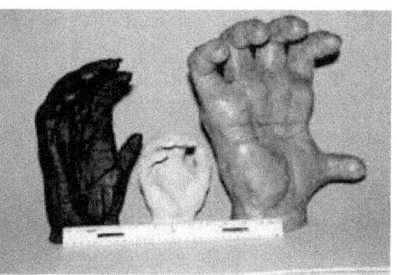

emales have breasts, small and conical near puberty (10-12 years, see data below), rather heavy nd pendulous during reproductive years and shrunken in old age. They are hair-covered except or the nipples and areolae.

he arms are massive and might exceed human length somewhat, frequently reported as hanging ose to their knees, though accentuated by the slouching stance of the animals. They are articularly hairy along the forearms and end in very large and massive hands (once described as he size of paddles").

he hand deviates in slight but significant ways from the human model (as derived from hand nd knuckle Fingers are generally shorter, especially the thumb, and the latter is carried "farther ward the wrist" as compared to the position in man. The hand largely lacks the thenar pad (the ounded muscle at the base of the thumb), a corollary of the lowest opposability found in the gher primates The hand is proportionately broader than that of man, palm width in adults easuring up to 8". Both finger and toe nails are deeply colored ("nicotine stained"), presumably combination of dirt and thick keratin, though fingernails are light colored in some. There are no aws.

oung males have a V-shaped trunk, tapering from a wide chest to a narrower waist, whereas the male trunk has an overall barrel shape. Female hips seem to be broader than those of the male.

Either sex rarely has a protruding abdomen (other than during pregnancy in the female). Genitalia in the female are hidden by hair, as are generally those of the male. The massive sexual swelling, observed in some female apes, has not been seen in the sasquatch.

Legs and Feet

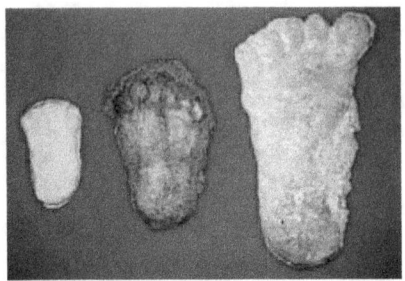

The legs are massive, especially the thighs, in one case reported to be the diameter of a "garbage can" (about 20"), but even in the (female) Patterson sasquatch about 15" thick. The calves are also unusually muscular, the gastrocnemius (calf) muscle being particularly prominent in rear views of the Patterson sasquatch.

Feet are most amply recorded by way of innumerable measured footprints. They range in recorded length from barely walking infants at 4"-5" to known female prints and very large presumptive male footprints The mean length of 702 prints (collected over nearly 50 years) is 15.6" with a range of 4" to 27", and a mean width of about 0.45 times that of the length. This proportion remains about the same with increasing length of the feet. Feet grow in excess of gain in height of the animals to compensate for the exponential increase in weight with linear dimensions. The foot does not have an arch, but retains the primitive primate midsole flexure of apes, called a metatarsal hinge. During running, often only the anterior half of the foot (anterior to the metatarsal hinge) contacts the ground The toes are capable of substantial splaying in lippery terrain, especially abduction of the big toe. The sole is very thick and indents deeply over uneven terrain without harm to the animal.

Body Size and Weight

The height average for the sampled population is 7' 10", derived from a combination of eye witness estimates and scaling from footprints. Babies shortly after birth are small (and "ugly", as one eye witness commented) by human standards, but grow rapidly and evidently walk at an early age. Aside from infants being carried, small walking sasquatches, 3-4' tall, have been seen. The animals reach maturity at a height of 6'-7' and the largest, reliably estimated individuals exceed 10'. Males are taller than females, but seemingly by no more than about a foot at the median of the population.

Weight is difficult to estimate on sight and seems to vary from animal to animal as much as in people, but a tight, established relationship exists in primates between chest circumference and weight. Applying this formula, the average sasquatch can be estimated to weigh 650 lbs the Patterson sasquatch 540 lbs, and the maximum (for a 24" or larger footprint) probably to exceed ,000 lbs.

That is some of the information that is how they look and what not. However, again, we do not know 100% if it is all true. We do know that they are really tall creatures. We do know that they are over 6 foot tall. We gathered all that information from eye witness accounts. Later on I will show you some accounts that people have said.

So how many different types are there? This question people been trying to answer. There really no true answer. We do know there are a few different types of creatures.

Bigfoot, Sasquatch, Yeti, Skunk Apes, Yowies, Almas, Kaptars & Mapinguari are just a few of it's many names. These large, bipedal apes occur in the folklore of native people across the globe. Here's a list of some of the most famous Bigfoot-like creatures.

Different Types of Bigfoot

SASQUATCH / BIGFOOT

"Sasquatch" is a derivative of "Sesquac," which means "wild man" in a British Columbian Native American language.

YETI

Stalking the high elevations of the Himalayas, the Yeti has captured the interest of the western world since climbers began tackling peaks like Everest. Local tribes consider the Yeti to be a fact of life, no more strange than the black bears of Appalachia. Reports from Western climbers are frequent throughout the last hundred years, so frequent that even Sir Edmund Hillary himself mounted an expedition in search of the massive man-ape.

ALMAS

Another variety of Bigfoot, this creature lives in the mountainous terrain on the border of Mongolia and China. It's more human-like than our Bigfoot; some scientists believe it's more of a Neanderthal than a primate.

SISIMITE

This is the ape-man of Central America. The shaggy-haired creature is said to have supernatural powers, which it uses to protect the wilderness. According to legend, the Sisimite will attack hunters in order to protect wildlife.

SKUNK APE

The Southernmost Bigfoot to occupy North America, the Skunk Ape is a resident of Florida's extensive Everglades. Some say it is a cousin to Bigfoot, while others say it's the same species. The number of sightings of the Skunk Ape in Florida rival the number sightings of Bigfoot in the Pacific Northwest. The animal earned its name because of its unique smell.

Even all these there are still more that have not been mentioned. There are so many different types. Here are 10 more types that you may want to know.

(3) Ten types of cryptic big foots.

1. The European Wildman

European folklore is rife with tales of the "Wild man of the Woods." They were so common tha

medieval heraldry often included depictions of the furry Wildmen. Aside from the fur, these

legends bear little resemblance to our modern Bigfoot stories, but some cryptozoologists still

speculate that they indicate the presence of hominid cryptids throughout the region.Unlike mos

Bigfoot stories, European Wildmen (and Wildwomen) could be basically any human (but most

often a hermit or eccentric to begin with) who wandered off to live in the woods. Living on

acorns and berries, they would grow fur all over their bodies and became less human with each

passing day. Stories about the Wildmen (sometimes called "Woodwose" or "Wooser") steadily

declined as Europe entered the modern age. However, Europeans did bring the legend with thei

to the New World. The first documented sighting of a Wildman in North America occurred in

1818, near Ellisburg, New York, when a "gentleman of unquestionable veracity" sighted a hair

covered man sprinting through the forest. Despite a huge search, no trace of the creature could l

found.Take Europe's Wildmen tales, transplant them to the New World, mix them with some

vaguely matching native beliefs, and you have a convincing explanation for the Bigfoot legend self. Whatever the truth, some cryptozoologists believe that the Wildman once existed but is ow extinct; laid low by the relentless advance of civilization.

The Nguoi Rung

he Nguoi Rung ("Forest People"), sometimes known as the "Batutut" or "Ujit," are hairy, ape-ke hominids said to inhabit the dense jungles of Vietnam, especially the Three Forests region, here Vietnam, Cambodia, and Laos converge. Descriptions vary in size, with fur ranging from ey to brown to a reddish color, but the creature is always said to walk in an upright, bipedal osition. By 1974, sightings had become so frequent that General Hoang Minh Thao, ommander of North Vietnamese forces in the Central Highlands, ordered a scientific survey of e area in an attempt to locate them. While an actual Nguoi Rung could not be located, the ientists did make a plaster cast of a suspiciously wide footprint.Possible candidates for the guoi Rung are Meganthropus, Homo erectus, or Neanderthal. A more controversial possibility was put forward by cryptozoologist Bernard Henvelmans, who suggested that the creature may be living examples of Homo pongoides—the infamous "Minnesota Iceman"—a supposed hominid, now widely believed to be a hoax, that was encased in ice and displayed at carnivals and fairs throughout the 1960s.

3. Lailoken, The Scottish Wildman

Scotland's version of the European Wildman legend is Lailoken, an insane oracle who lived in the forests near what is now Glasgow in the late sixth century AD. He is referenced in The Life of Saint Kentigern where he is described as, "a certain foolish man, who was called Laleocen." Like most European Wildman tales, he was often described as covered in hair and wearing ragged animal skins.The most interesting thing about the madman of southern Scotland is his association with Merlin. A medieval text known as the Scotichronicon gives an account of ailoken's life that is almost identical to the Welsh legends of Myrddin Wyllt, one of the orerunners of the Arthurian Merlin.

The Yeren

he Yeren, also known as the Shennongjiayerenn (we'll stick to Yeren), is a bigfoot-type cryptid ought to inhabit China, particularly the Shennongjia region of northwestern Hubei province. escriptions vary—some legends describe short creatures with entirely hairy bodies, while hers describe giants with grayish-red hair and a mix of human and ape-like features. These scriptions have led many investigators to conclude that the legends actually describe bears, bbons, and a variety of other rare animals known to inhabit the region.Still, legends of the eren go back centuries. The Ch'ing dynasty poet, Yuan Mei (1716–98), described a creature hich is "monkey-like, yet not a monkey." A much older legend states that during the time of e first Chinese Emperor people would run off to the woods to avoid forced labor on the Great

Wall. Like the Wildmen of Europe, these fugitives would grow fur over their bodies and become wild. A legend containing a grain of truth, perhaps?Modern sightings of the Yeren have been fairly prolific. In 1940, a biologist named Wang Tselin supposedly studied the body of a female Yeren. In 1976, a group of six bureaucrats described an encounter with a Yeren on an isolated road in Hubei province, prompting an official expedition to look for evidence (locals provided fur and feces supposedly belonging to the creature, but no direct evidence).One of the most recent sightings was a 2007 incident when four tourists found themselves "almost face to face" with two of the creatures deep in the Shennongjia Nature Reserve.

5. Pakistan's Barmanu

In the remote wilderness of eastern Afghanistan and Pakistan's Shishi Kuh Valley there may live a human-like creature known as the Barmanu ("Hairy One"). The creature's range places it smack in the middle of the region where the better-known Yeti and Alma are thought to live (an may be that all three are one and the same).The Barmanu was first brought to the outside world's attention by Spanish cryptozoologist Jordi Magraner, who described it as resembling a Neanderthal, sometimes wearing animal skins, and possessed of an especially foul stench. This description is notably similar to America's legendary "Skunk Ape."Magraner and a team of investigators traveled regularly to the region between 1992 and 1994, reporting footprints and grunting sounds in the night (which they attributed to a "primitive voice box"). Magraner continued his research, but on August 2, 2002, tragedy struck when he was murdered by his Pakistani guide just a few weeks before he had planned to return to Europe with his findings.Interestingly, when Magraner showed eyewitnesses illustrations of various real and alleged hominids, the picture they consistently chose was one of the "Minnesota Iceman"

The Alma Of Mongolia

Probably the most famous cryptid on this list is the Alma (Mongolian for "Wildman") which hails from the Altai Mountains of southern Mongolia. Professor Boris Porchnev of the Moscow Academy of Sciences used eyewitness accounts to put together this composite description of the beast: "There is no underlayer of hair so that the skin can sometimes be seen. The head rises to a cone-shaped peak . . . the teeth are like a man's, but larger, with the canines more widely separated." Porchnev's description also noted that the Alma could run as fast as a horse. Breeding pairs lived together in underground burrows, eating small animals and vegetables and emerging at night. Similar to the Barmanu, the Alma is noted for a "distasteful smell." Because there are so many older, traditional tales of the Alma and similar creatures among the peoples of Central Asia, these sightings of humanoid cryptids bring up the interesting possibility that early humans may have interacted with still-surviving versions of primitive hominids. When asked about this possibility in a USA Today article (after an intriguing pinky bone was found in a Siberian cave that was only 30,000 years old), folklorist Michael Heaney noted that such legends have been known in the area for centuries. "The reports of wild men, although having typical mythic overtones, do often reflect what we know of primitive hominins. The presumed [Almas] of Central Asia could be any one of a number of pre-sapien ancestors."

The Urayuli Of Southwest Alaska

Within the vast forests that surround Alaska's Lake Iliamna it is said that a mysterious hominid-like creature lurks, reaching three meters (10 ft) in height and covered in dark, shaggy hair. Sightings of the creature have been fairly regular, with one as recently as 1999, when a group discovered huge tracks along the bank of Belkofski Bay. In the same year, an eyewitness claimed to have seen a gigantic ape-like creature with extremely long arms standing on two legs. Terrifyingly, the creature was described as standing over 4 meters (13 ft) in height. It is unlikely that the creature, if it exists, is any kind of hominid survival, since none are known to have reached such gigantic heights.Like similar legends about Wildmen, it is said that children who wander off into the woods and get lost transform into Urayuli. Legend also has it that they emit a haunting cry, like that of a loon.

8. The Nittaewo

This diminutive race of "beast-men" were described by Pliny the Elder in the first century AD as a tribe living in modern Sri Lanka, side by side with a people known as the Veddahs. The Veddahs themselves turned out to be very real, and possessing their own legends about the Nittaewo. The legends claim that the Veddahs were responsible for eliminating the entire Nittaewo race (long feared by the Veddahs for their cruelty), which they trapped in a cave. The Veddahs then piled firewood around the entrance of the cave and set it alight, causing the remaining Nittaewo to suffocate from the smoke. The Veddah myths describe the Nittaweo as orangutan-like climbers a little over a meter (3 ft) tall and covered in dark red fur. Their voices were said to be like the twittering of birds. Similar to the Alma, many cryptozoologists believe that these legends describe a cryptid hominid still living among modern humans within recorded history, but going extinct before it could be documented. Yet in 1887, British explorer Hugh Nevill documented tales of more recent warfare between the two tribes (although again the Nittaewo were supposed to be extinct by the time Nevill came along). He reportedly learned from a family of Veddah lineage that the Nittaewo were exterminated four generations earlier, around 1775, and that a relative of the family had actually taken part in burning their last home the 1940s, British primatologist W.C. Osman Hill concluded, based on descriptions and some ther flimsy evidence, that the Nittaewo must be Homo erectus. Later, in 1963, Captain A.T. ambukwella theorized that the Nittaewo may have been a species of Australopithecus (the mous "Hobbit" hominid) based on its reputed small size.

The Honey Island Swamp Monster

ack in the 1970s and '80s, the Honey Island Swamp region of Louisiana became briefly famous the home of a bipedal man-creature dubbed the "Honey Island Swamp Monster," the outhern-Fried Bigfoot," or simply "the Thing." The rumors were started by two hunters, arlan E. Ford and Billy Mills, who claimed to have seen the beast and presented plaster casts of footprints (which they allege were found next to a wild boar carcass with its throat slashed). nlike most hominid cryptid encounters, these casts indicated a creature with four web-toed pendages, prompting some to theorize that the creature was some kind of cross between a hominid and an alligator or lizard. Reports quickly escalated in a state where every county and village has its own legends and monsters, and soon the Honey Lake region gained nationwide notoriety. There are some older legends that seem to justify the existence of the creature (or maybe "inspired" them). Local Native American tribes have a legend of a creature called the "Letiche," a semi-aquatic "man-beast" raised by alligators in the depths of the swamps. Cajun legends of the "Loup Carou" may be referring to a creature similar to the Honey Island sighting rather than the (mistaken) notion that they are werewolves. The strangest of them all is a ludicrous local story about a train wreck that accidentally unleashed a cage full of chimpanzees—who then moved into the swamp and interbred with alligators! The Honey Island Swamp Monster was one of the major inspirations for "Lockjaw," the monster featured in the 2011 horror movie, Creature.

10. Siberia's Chuchunaa

The Chuchunaa ("outcast," or "fugitive"), also known as the Tjutjuna, is a hominid cryptid rumored to live in the snowy depths of Siberia. Described as almost 2 meters (6 ft) tall, with protruding brows, long matted hair, and a full beard, many people believe them to be surviving Neanderthal or Homo gardarensis. Unusually for such legends, the Chuchunaa was commonly reported to wear clothing made of deer skin. In 1933, Professor P. Dravert, after hearing account that the Chuchunaa were being hunted, petitioned the Soviet government to put an end to the practice, calling for the creatures to be recognized as full citizens of the Soviet Union and therefore deserving of equal rights under the law. His call to action went unheeded at the time, but as recently as 1970, geologist Vladimir Pushkarev was conducting research on the creatures concluding that their numbers were dwindling as civilization encroached on their territory. Once reported so often that the Soviet government was fairly convinced of their existence, there have een only a few modern sightings of the creature, mostly unreliable or unsubstantiated, and a few f the standard blurry/shaky videos, such as the one above, have surfaced on YouTube. Some ports insist that the Chuchunaa are man-eaters and that they have a tendency to steal food and upplies from campsites. Despite a wealth of tales from throughout history, no physical evidence f any kind has been found to support the Chuchunaa legend.

'ell that is pretty much all I was able to find online. Now to answer that one question "What uppened on some encounters of the Big Foot"? Well here are a few statements that people have aid that happened.

ncounters of Big Foot (4)

1. Belen, New Mexico, September 1999

[anzano Mountain Range

i Bobbie, my name is Daniel Jaramillo. I live in Belen, New Mexico. I have a story to tell you. oday I was riding my four-wheeler with my friend. We were on one of my favorite trails when y friend saw something big and black. She said she saw it twice and that she thought it was just r imagination. Well, we left that trail and went on yet another one of my favorite trails.

'e were turning around to head back when I saw what she had seen. We stopped first to get a tter look to see if I wasn't imagining it. Then I was got very scared because it looked like it w us. I put the throttle on my four-wheeler all the way to get out of the woods. When I looked the right of us I noticed that it was running along side us about some distance, maybe 70 feet vay. I was terrified and since then I haven't gone out on my four-wheeler. The creature was big, hairy and husky like a football player. The terrain was rocky and yet very green loose rocks everywhere. The creature also had a look that scared both me and my friend. It looked like it knew what we were going to do. This happened in the Manzano Mountains in New Mexico around 5:45 pm MT. This report was near the Manzano Mountain Range, which is situated in the wooded foothills of the Manzano (the Spanish word for apple) Mountains State Park. The Manzano Mt. Range encompasses 36,970 acres on the Mountainair Ranger District of the Cibola National Forest and is located in Belen's backyard. (Belen sits to the east of I-25 south of Albuquerque, NM.) Accessible trails lie on both sides of the mountain and picnic areas abound. Wilderness elevations range from 6,000 feet in the foothills to 10,098 feet on Manzano Peak. The district office is in Mountainair where advice on trails and recreation is offered. It is a popular place for fishing, bird watching, photography, hiking, and cross-country skiing.

2. Mora County, New Mexico

I had submitted a report recently, and then gotten cold feet when those other investigators tried to speak with me, due to a personal dilemma. I will explain in detail, but I have had alot of time to think about different aspects and other incidents. Let me start at the beginning. My name is John V.

My grandfather, who has recently passed away, owned an 1100-acre ranch along coyote creek. Approximately xx miles out side of Mora County, New Mexico. The first incident occurred in about 1968 or 1969. According to my uncle who's nickname is Leroy. He is known to be an exaggerator, so I never really new if he was telling the truth, until I had my own experiences. Any way he was on a camping trip during that summer, with his hippie friends, two girls and one guy. They had set up a tent to sleep in and started a campfire, and ate dinner.

ıst after dark my uncle, and his male friend were both Vietnam veterans had began to ʳag in front of these girls about who was the strongest, and most fearless, and so on, any ʳay it had gotten pretty late, probably around midnight, as Leroy recalled and he said to ɪs friend, if your such a tough guy why don't you walk across the creek, and up the side f the mountain in the pitch black of the night, and when you get about half way up, sleep ıere by your self for the remainder of the night, he said you can take your sleeping bag, ut nothing else, and his friend replied no problem, since he had been a green beret, and ʳas afraid so he claimed of nothing. So he grabbed his sleeping bag, and set out in the ark. Just as he agreed, and proceeded about half way up the mountain, where he laid own to sleep. Then approximately about 3 a.m. my uncle, and the girls woke to a ɔrribly loud scream that he had never heard before in his life. He said it was eerie, ɔmewhere between a roar and a scream. He was so terrified that he grabbed a shovel, ıd jumped out of the tent to see if he could see anything. It was still dark but he could ɛe something coming down the mountain hobbling, and approaching his tent very ıpidly. He clenched the shovel and was getting ready to swing, when he heard the voice f his friend saying, "it's me, it's me."" He was still in his mummy bag. My uncle asked ım what happened, and he said a giant creature had walked up to where he was sleeping, ı two legs. He said it was covered with hair, and roared at him. He got so scared; he dn't have time to get out of his sleeping bag. He told Leroy we should get the hell out of ɛre so they loaded up the camp, and drove off as fast as they could!

he next incident was an experience my grandfather had. It was about 1973 or 1974. He ıd cattle and he drove out about once a month to check on them. He had a small cabin ɛar the creek. He would often take me with him we were very close, and had a special sort of bond. We would have long talks, and really got to know each other. Any way we went to spend a weekend at the cabin, so he could do his routine. We got there in the evening, ate dinner, and went to bed he always got up at 4 in the morning, before the sun came up and set out across the creek, to cut wild loco weed, so the cows would not eat it. I would stay in bed till about 8 a.m., when he would return and make breakfast. Well tha morning he retuned about 5 a.m., woke me and looked white as a ghost I new him well, and he was a man that was not afraid of anything, he said he was cutting loco weed at precisely the crack of dawn, when he heard a scream that made the skin crawl up the bac of his neck. It was unlike anything he had ever heard. He said at first he thought it sounded like a woman's scream, but there was something animal like, it was very hard fc him to describe. This was a man who was raised on this very mountain and had visited time and time again, but never recalled anything like it.

The men got together for a game of cards, and beer on the picnic tables. The women wer inside the cabin to gossip. My brother and sister were playing together. My cousin Freddie and me were bored, and we approached my grandfather. He said I have the cure for you, and quickly put us to work. He had a ten acre corral, fenced with barbed wire, surrounding a fruit orchard. What he wanted us to do was take these wire twists, and insert them between the posts, binding the barbed wire through the twists. So we took as many twists as we could carry, and my dog, and set out to the southwest corner of the corral.

There were no cows, because they were on top of the mesa grazing. It was a beautiful clear and warm day I told my cousin, we'd start at this corner you work west toward the fruit orchard, and ill work the fence north. My dog stayed at my side, as I worked north.

bout 30 minutes into it my dog started acting very strange. I was trying to continue orth, but he would not move. He was frozen stiff, belly and nose down in the dirt, facing est directly towards the fruit orchard. His eyes were tearing, which I had never seen efore, and he was letting out a very quiet whimpering, which I had never seen before. I icked and pulled at him to try to get him to move, but he would not budge. Then I could ear a heavy breathing, very low pitched rumbling, and then a long loud low-pitched ar, coming directly from the fruit orchard. I looked, and I saw what I thought was a ear. I could still hear it breathing I looked closer, focusing my eyes, and noticed it was tting down like a man, on a knocked over tree, as it was eating apples with one hand, ill breathing heavy, but yet it seemed to be looking directly at me, and I got the feeling was happy, and somehow smiling at me. At that moment, my cousin had reached me at reak neck speed, yelling did you here that? I replied I'm looking at it. He turned to look; e saw it stand from its sitting position, next to a 12-foot apple tree. It seemed to be just tall as the tree, or pretty close reaching in grabbing apples with one arm, one at a time, en sit and eat one at a time, while staring at us every time it ate one. It was covered in ng reddish hair all over its body; the sun shining directly on it its hair. It almost seemed have blondish sun bleached highlights very shiny. It had a cone shaped head and it oked clean. I personally wasn't scared, but my cousin was frantic, and the way my dog as acting troubled me. My cousin said were dead I replied look at the length of its legs, e are standing about 200 yards away I think if it really wanted to hurt us, we would ready be dead, and he replied I'm not taking any chances, I'm gonna make a run for it. I id if your running I'm not staying so we took one last look, and darted, and my dog got and darted after us.

We ran as fast as we could to the cabin, where my dad, grandfather, godfather, and they're friends, were playing poker, and drinking beer. We ran up screaming frantically there's some sort of creature in the fruit orchard. My grandfather replied you guys are jus trying to get out of work dammit. Get back to work. Nobody would believe us so I told my little brother, and he said I want to see it. Show me. He grabbed a hand full of bottle rockets, and we walked towards the orchard. To his amazement, and ours the creature was still there eating apples.

My brother started shooting bottle rockets at it. I told him not to but he did not listen, the the creature casually stood up from its sitting position, and gracefully walked deeper into the orchard, out of our view. We told my brother to walk over into the orchard, to see if i was still there, and he replied no way! We knew no one would ever believe us. So we pu it behind us, and just tried to forget about it. We would talk about it amongst each other, but never to any one else, out of fear of ridicule.

Years went by! The next incident happened in the winter of 95 about mid November. I was anxious to start my own business, selling live trees. I had a small Mazda pickup my grandfather was loaning me. I got my nursery license, tree tags, some twine, some burlap some nails, chicken wire, a bailing hook, a shovel, and two spades. My idea was to collect Pinon pines and juniper from my grandfather's ranch, bring it to Albuquerque, an sell it on the side of the road.

I was married then, my son only seven years old, so my wife and son stayed in town, while I ventured out on the weekends to collect trees. Always the same set of circumstances. I chose an area with loose soil, however there is an abundance of mineral in this 80-acre area, off of the main dirt road. It's pristine, virtually untouched virgin land ut definitely a mineralologists dream. It had heavy pine Pinon, and juniper in the lower

evation, and Douglas fir white fir in the upper region. The minerals I've come across

hile digging up trees I've seen huge chunks of pyrite fall from the root balls as I dig

em out. Copper azurite silver white quarts flint and many others I don't even know the

ames of, but a rock collectors dream.

nyway back to my point, I drive my truck into this certain area as far as I can until the

ees become so thick I have to stop and set out on foot. I grab my backpack with all my

ear including food and water, and one shovel, and a spade, no guns I don't believe in

em! I walk about 300-600 yards into the forest. Looking for only the best looking tree

ecimens I can find, one here, one there spread out. I'll locate one set down my gear,

ke a drink of water, take a deep breath of fresh air, relax, and break out my favorite

pe, and then start to dig.

bout 15 minutes into it I get a strange sensation. A distinct feeling that I am being

atched I look into the trees and I can see movement from tree to tree, at several points,

various locations, about two hundred yards, but the figures are shadowy, and hard to

cus on, but they seem to be large upright, moving from behind the tree to another tree.

'ell I figure maybe my minds just playing tricks on me, so I continue with my work, I'll

llect all my trees, lift the root balls, and drag them back to my truck, and call it a day;

ive back to Albuquerque, and return ever other weekend or so that winter with the

entical circumstances. I told my wife and she didn't know what to make of it.

he summer came and I didn't return till the next winter in 96. That first winter was dry,

d there was no snow, but the next winter was moist. I started again in November this time it was snowing quite heavy. I did the same routine but this time there was virgin snow.

I got out of the truck at the usual location, but walking through fresh snow my foot print visible I walked out, did my usual routine, about 15 minutes into digging I get the same sensation I am being watched but this time I for sure can clearly see a figure in the trees, very visible because every thing is white and this figure is dark but I try not to pay to much attention and continue my work once all my trees are ready, I grab the first two; one root ball in each hand, and ! drag them towards the truck following the exact foot prints I made earlier.

About halfway to the truck I saw foot prints directly crossing my path about 15 to 18 inches in length very large with 3 toes a left foot and a right foot one large toe on each a medium toe and a smaller toe about 7 to 8 feet a part I wonder could this be the same creature I had seen when I was a child? I return several weekends in a row that same winter, in fresh snow with the exact same circumstances.

I told my wife and she definitely believed me but who else would believe me? I thought So I called my brother I told him the story and suggested it could be the same creature w had seen when we were kids. He remembered the incident but still he said my current story sounded a bit hard to believe.

So I said there is only one way to find out, and asked if he would go to the area the following weekend. He agreed we went together that weekend, and I did every thing the same it was snowing really hard when we got there.

So we sat in the truck til it died down, then got out together only our tracks in the snow, walked out about 300 yards started to dig, I figured we would take turns I told him to tart digging he went about 10 minutes, and then I went about 10 minutes, and then he

aid he had the incredible sensation, I felt it to, we looked out, and saw what seemed to

e twenty or so figures watching and moving about 100 yards in a half circle in the

erimeter.

e was terrified I told him not to be, as animals have been known to sense fear. I told

im to relax I gave him a drink of water, and we both smoked my pipe we continued our

ork, started gathering our equipment, and trees, followed our foot prints out I expected

 see tracks as I had before and we did but I was astounded, For the first time I saw three

ets of 3 toed prints the large set I had seen before but a smaller set and even smaller set I

ooked at him and said oh my God there must be family's of these creatures.

thought we should have brought some plaster because no one will ever believe us, but at

e same time I was relieved, because I had at least one real witness and if nothing else. I

new I wasn't imagining these incidents! I'm sure I could have gathered even more proof,

ut my father wanted me to stop digging up trees, in fear that I might damage the

nvironment he told my grandmother to pull the plug on my tree business, and my

randfather took the truck! I've recently passed through the area during the summer

onths and have had the same being watched sensations. I know they're out there!

ack to my dilemma I spoke of at the beginning, I feel like I'm caught between science,

d nature. on one hand I feel it's my duty to reveal this because it may be of great

portance to science, and mankind. On the other hand I feel these creatures have never

ought any harm to me, and I owe it to them to preserve protect they're safe haven. I

ve to look at all the angles. Man by nature wants to ultimately prove he is the smartest

 all species. To do this he has exploited caged and zoo every other species on the planet as specimens of a lower intellect, somehow giving himself a sense of empowerment and dominion over other species.

What exactly would happen if we could absolutely prove Bigfoot exists? Would the Bigfoot benefit or would we benefit? Would we get rich, would we be famous, would we have a moment of glory?

What would the Bigfoot gain? Why has Bigfoot eluded mankind for so long? There must be a reason? With all the reported sightings I would think it's pretty obvious that it exists. Isn't that enough?

My own personal experience suggests to me that bigfoot is trying to communicate something to us and that is symbolic, mutual respect for all living creatures. By hunting them down, aren't we just forcing them to run further away? Maybe we should just leave well enough alone! What do you think? For the sake of science I am willing to take a lie detector test to back my claims my brother is also willing. I have not spoken to my cousin in years but I am sure I could persuade him to take the test also.

John

3. **Apache County, Arizona**

   November 2000

   Nearest road is 164, Chinle Navajo Nation

   Closest water: Wheatfield Lake, Chuska Mountains

   The creature was strange in color. It wasn't the usual brown or black. It was actually dark orange and white. I was shocked and confused. I didn't know these things existed around my area, but I also didn't know that they are colorful. It was about a foot taller than me; I am 6'2". It is about 7 feet tall. It appeared old and saggy-like; smart by its facial expression. It kind of seemed like it was better than me or something. It smelled really bad, I thought a skunk was around. There are coniferous trees about and grass and rocks. This sighting had taken place in a mountainous area, a valley to be precise. Only my family knows about this.

Have there been other sightings in Arizona, especially in the Navajo Nation area?

Willippa Hills, near Grays River, Washington

off Hwy. 101 - November 1978 after 4:30 pm.

The terrain was described as remote old growth timber, with deep carpet of pine needles, beside a small river, just around dark. Closest water source: River, tributary of Grays River. My self and my hunting partner, whom I will call DW was hunting elk in this area, which was old growth timber, about 3-4 miles from the nearest logging road.

We had started early that morning and had jumped a large herd of elk which contained several large bulls, but were unable to get a shot. We decided that we would wait until the late afternoon when the elk returned to this area, as we wanted the large 5-point bull that was in that herd. Since we were using muzzle-loaders, or black powder rifles we knew that we wanted a close shot so we stayed down by the river as to conceal ourselves.

Well the elk never showed, so we had just started our hike out of the timber, following the river as there was more daylight showing. I was in the lead, going around a tree in the trail when I came face to face with a large creature, with bright red eyes, which were at least 24 inches over my head. The creature turned and was out of sight in less than 30 seconds, and boy was I scared. DW and I still had at least 2 more miles to hike out, and this was the same way the creature had fled.

We both decided to give this thing some time to clear out of the area before we started t

leave. Needless to say we were extremely glad to get back to the truck that evening. The

creature we both saw was at least 7 feet tall, possibly more, had bright red eyes, which

kind of glowed in the near dark light conditions that we were in. This creature which

turned in front of me less than 6 feet away, was a real hulk, big barrel-chested, massive

arms and shoulders, and the really impressive fact was it never made a sound when it

turned to leave, it just seemed to float away. It was very hard to keep calm, but I knew

almost as soon as I saw those red eyes what this creature must be. I have hunted and

fished this country for years and have never had anything like this happen before, but I

truly wish I could see him again, and may yet.

We have only told a few friends what happened that evening, and only tonight I felt

compelled to write to your email address to share this story with others, whom may hav

similar experiences but choose to keep them to themselves. I urge you to let others kno

of your sightings, DW, and myself know what we saw, and are more certain everyday

that all of the outdoorsmen, hunters, fishermen, and etc. share the forests with these

creatures.

5. Adams County, Pennsylvania

    May 2001

    11:40 PM, Near Rte. 15

    Our yard to its rear has a drain that is able to be climbed down into. The grate comes o

    easily and my teenage son can climb down into it and walk under the development. It i

    cemented and it leads to the creek. I am wondering if this thing knows about this route

    The land is wooded to the east and north. the city of Gettysburg lies to the south and est. The South Mountain range is located west of Gettysburg. Looking on a PA map ne can see the South Mountains as a part of a group of ranges of mountains that lie most parallel to each other stretching from the Northwest. On the sightings page I oticed that Bigfoot have been spotted in Westmoreland County which is west of Adams ounty. A co-worker said that he spotted a bigfoot walking through his boy scout ampground in very large strides one night in 1985. It was in Mt. Newville or Newville ea.

ack to my home, there is a creek to my south about 1/2 mile away. On occasion I have potted a blue heron fishing in it so I know that fish exist in it. Slightly hilly would be n accurate description. The new high school is built near here and there are farms with ees and wooded areas north of here (2 miles away and beyond). The nearest city is ettysburg. I saw a 6' black creature that moved back beside my garage. I smelled the tten fish smell mixed with garbage smell in my 150' tall blue spruce while exiting my hicle in the driveway.

vish to remain anonymous. For the past four years that I have lived in this velopment I have spent some time late at night watching TV. I am alone by my living om window and I often feel like something is watching me. My husband and I are ture buffs and do not have a light on outside the house. Our yard is not chemically eated nor do we fertilize our lawn. We often see hawks and moles and toads and other nall creatures that seem almost extinct in the other yards in the area with their dogs, ts, fences, chemically treated grass and other natural obstacles.

vo summers ago the plants under my bedroom window have been trampled on verely, as if something were looking through the window at us. We wondered if there was a large dog in the yard. Occasionally we have found what looks like dog feces in our backyard garden plot (surrounded by 1 ¼ foot high metal fencing. I was wondering who would let their dog out that late to roam. Over the years we have heard noises outside our window and evidence of what appears to be a great animal of weight. Our small evergreen bushes have also been compressed as if someone was sitting on top of them, especially those under the bedroom window.

On the night of May 15 2001 I drove home late from a church meeting with friends. It was 11:40 AM. We have a huge blue spruce tree in our front yard (150' high easy). My son once cut a few limbs on the back of it so he and a friend could make a little play area. I often worried that someone could be lurking in it. I got out of my car in the driveway, which is 2' away from the blue spruce and the next thing I knew I was overcome with the most nauseating smell like something is rotten. I have never experienced this before here and wondered if someone had dropped garbage on our lawn. It was rather late so I hastily looked around the ground and did not approach the tree where it emanated from the strongest. I walked towards the garage and the smell diminished so I knew it was coming from the tree. I did see a black figure by the garage when I pulled up but it shrank back towards the garage. I wondered what it was but was too afraid to investigate. Since I am a female I did not pursue on foot. This time I did not bother my husband but hastily walked towards the door. I remember the smell of the thing in the tree as of rotten fish. We live less than a mile from a part of Rock Creek and I was wondering if this creature had eaten recently.

At 5:20 AM on May 16 2001 I was curious about this event. I went out to water my garden and around the house. We have two identical red maples in our back yard and he one had no twigs down around the bottom. For Mother's Day we had cut our grass

nd meticulously I had picked up every twig in the back yard. Imagine my surprise

hen I noticed a perfect circle of fallen small end-of- branch twigs laying completely

round the red maple at the left of the house nearest the blue spruce and, then, no twigs

round the other red maple? I went in to tell my husband. The twigs were broken at

ast 9' above my head around the tree. Each twig was very thin. They looked as if they

ere snapped off and not cut by a precision instrument. My garage is open at night and I

ent in to check my pruner. It was behind another tool and appeared to be unused. I

ent out to check the blue spruce.

his time, on the side where my son had sawed a few branches, I saw a number of

roken twigs and branches above my head appearing to extend about 9' above the

round. If this thing is a Bigfoot, which I think it is, then, I was wondering if it can be

aught on infrared light photography? Also, I have read that they abduct humans at

me--is this when one is approached in the wilds and not in a suburban setting? There

ay have been two for the one I saw by the garage was about 6' at the most. Could this

ave been an offspring?

wo weeks ago we put large items on our back porch that is usually clear other times.

uring the evening of the day we had moved the items, about 12:00 AM, there was a

ud noise that came from the back porch where the items were placed. I thought at the

ne that something must have had a routine for coming onto our back porch and did not

ow that we had just put some large items out. When I turned on the light I saw

thing. On other occasions there have been sounds and when I turn on the light and

ok I am always wondering why I don't see a large dog or skunk in the vicinity to

justify the sounds because I do go out and check immediately in the yard for about 20'
with a flashlight. I have not seen a raccoon although opossums seem to live in the
woods (highway road kill attests to this).

6. Summers County, West Virginia

February 2001 near Rt 20 not far from Bluestone lake, nearest city - Hinton 2001
The terrain was very brushy, I was walking down a mountain when I came cross the
creature in a creek bed. I would estimate the creature to have been about 7ft tall and
weighing close to 400 or 500lbs. The arms were very long and swinging with the
movement. There wasn't any hair on its face, the skin was a very dark brown. The eyes
were small black and round. It walked upright with an almost comical gate, it had a
slight slouch. What I saw was a large humanoid creature walking like a human being.
When the creature saw me it slowly and calmly walked away. There was no aggression
in the animal at all. Its face was quite ape like but didn't protrude out at the mouth. I wa
about 30 yards from the creature whenever we saw each other.

7. (5) Mr. C's Nevada sasquatch encounter:

My Stepdad and I left Reno headed for Northern Elko County and the Jarbidge
Mountains for his archery Mule Deer hunt he had drawn early on the morning of Augu
6, 2014. It took about 7 hours to get there as we had to finish some shopping for
perishable food items we needed. We really didn't have a set return date for this trip we
just planned on staying out there until we had had enough or the season ended. During
the 7 days leading up to us leaving Northern Elko County was just getting hammered
with rain and thunderstorms every day. The day before we left I had read that where w
were headed had received 4.5 inches of rain in 6 days, which for the desert is a ton of

water. There were areas up there that were currently flooding at the time we left and much of the northern area of the county was under flood advisories.

We really didn't know what to expect up there and the forecast just kept calling for more thunderstorms every day pretty much around the clock. We were there for a total of 12 days and 9 of those days it rained heavily when the thunderstorms rolled through. It turns out while we were there it rained almost another 6 inches in 9 days. It was a very soggy trip but I tell you this to give you an idea of the great tracking conditions we were presented with if you could find any tracks before the rain got to them.

We arrived at camp a little after 2pm on the 6th. By the looks of it nobody else had been on any of the roads we traveled to get back to our camp. With as wet as it was it would have been very evident if they had. We got stuck several times trying to get back to the camp. The season started on the 10th but we showed up early to get some good scouting time in before then. We set up a few quick things unloaded the side by side and hit the trails. This was my stepdad"s first trip into this particular unit and he was very anxious to see what country was available to us.

We scouted around until 7ish and returned to set up camp enough to keep us dry if it turned to raining that night. While doing that I noticed a broken tree I had not noticed before. I went over to check it out and was immediately taken aback by it. I was looking at a healthy tree that was still alive except for the broken part that had been bent over 90 degrees and snapped with no damage to any other part of the tree or trees that were surrounding it. It had not been hit by lightning or hit by a truck or ATV or anything like that. I don't know if it's worth noting but the broken part was pointing at the camp site. Needless to say I felt I was looking at my first tree break. I had no other explanation for it and it definitely happened that year during the growing season as the tree had fully leafed out before it was broken. I've used this camp site 3 years in a row now and it definitely was not there in the previous trips. The tree was roughly 3 inches in diameter give or take and could not have been an easy break. I got my stepdad to help me try to replicate it on other trees of similar size and accomplished nothing. The tree species was a quaking aspen.

After that we ate dinner and set up our cots on the back of the trailer for the side by side, tarped it off really nice to keep us dry and got ready for bed. This is the time I started to feel not right about the situation. I got that nagging feeling of dread and of being watched. The rain had stopped for the last few hours and it was dead silent. In the 3 years I've been there I've never heard it that quiet, it was that deafening quiet. Ever since my first sasquatch experience I always have my flash light and gun by my side at night with no exceptions and tonight would be no different. I had left both in the truck and realized it right before I climbed into my bag for the night so I climbed out of our trailer tarp setup to retrieve them.

By now we were between two thunder cells and the lightning was flashing occasionally lighting everything up. The truck was about 10-12 yards from the trailer. When I reached the passenger side right as I was about to open the door, lightning flashed and 6-7 yards in front of me was the silhouetted figure of an upright standing two legged hairy man with a slight conical shape to the head. It appeared that it was going from right to left and not directly facing me and then it all went black and an eerie thunder crackled. I must have damn near torn the truck door off the hinges I felt I was moving so fast to get my light and gun, I was freaking out at that point. I mean see something 20 feet from me and have the lights go out like that and see how calm you can stay.

Anyhow, I got my light and gun and saw nothing there when I got the light on which was maybe a second or two later so now armed I felt a little braver and walked over to the road I thought I saw it on and did find some tracks going from right to left. The trouble with that though is that we had walked all over that area and they all looked very similar with no definitive toes. It was just all a bunch of mushed looking prints because it was beyond muddy, most areas had no firmness left to the dirt and mud it was just a boggy mess. So I half ass convince myself that I'm seeing things from the long day I've had and am letting that tree break get to my head a little too much.

I walk back while scrutinizing the entire 360 degrees around camp very carefully with my flashlight and climb into bed. I'll never forget looking at my phone to see the time when I climbed in to my sleeping bag. It was 9:02pm. I shut the phone off and laid there thinking about where and what I might show my stepdad the next day. What began to happen next is what has turned me from a complete skeptic to a complete believer of the Sasquatch.

was 10-15 minutes tops, from when I laid down and I started hearing movement outside the p and began hearing the squishing of the mud under something's feet. It was moving very althily and came up to within a few feet of the tarp directly behind my head and stopped. I'm ng there trying to decipher the sound I just heard and the tarp starts being pushed down at my d section. It was pushed down about a foot and me not thinking at all and really freaking out the inside without making noise on the outside reacted and swatted at the pushed down area d hit something pretty hard that hurt my hand. The tarp went back up immediately and what is standing there shuffled back and smacked the tarp directly behind my head causing me to let t an "AHHHHHH!!!!!!" sound and I consequently re-chambered a round into my Glock .45.

Before I go any farther I need to let people know that my stepdad was on the same trailer about 8 feet from me lightly snoring from time to time and that he is probably the soundest sleeper I've ever met. I'm convinced he could sleep through the house burning down and a carpet bombing a block away. The way we had the tarp setup was like a burrito with his en tied closed and my side being the open end to climb out of. So now I'm lying there with my gun ready after it slapped the tarp behind my head and it goes dead silent.

I'm not sure how much time goes by during these silent periods. it could be as much as 5 or 10 minutes but I soon hear the one behind me move a little and hear more coming up to the side m stepdad is on. I know there was two of them that came up on his side because two opposite corners of the tarp began getting pulled on at the same time and smacked around. All the while still have the one behind me and my stepdad is happily asleep. This is the point where everyone always asks me why didn't you wake up your stepdad and why didn't you start shooting? Well I was trying to wake him up. I would call out his name as loud as I felt comfortable because whe these things heard you it would amp them up and they would shake the trailer and slap and pull the tarp.

Now as far as shooting goes I wanted to in the worst way, however I couldn't see what I was shooting at and I only had 13 rounds on me I left my other clip in the truck. Knowing there was of them outside I didn't feel shooting would accomplish anything except maybe getting us both killed. I felt the gun probably wasn't big enough to do the job unless I had a clean head shot or two and it was almost pitch black with the moon just starting to rise. Not to mention I had a ma asleep that had no idea anything was happening. If I were to have shot at one and they really attacked he never would have stood a chance and I would never want to put a family member o nybody for that matter in that situation. They hadn't tried to come in and I felt it was a scare actic to get us to come out.

o that crap keeps going on for a while, and I keep trying to wake my stepdad to no avail. During ne of the silent periods the one behind me started to urinate just feet from my head. That put a hole new scared into me for some reason. The volume had to be 2 or 3 times that of a man rinating. to me it sounded like a horse or a big bull urinating. I also need to say that the tarp was ver 7 feet off the ground were this thing pushed down on it earlier. I couldn't do it and I'm 6'3" d 305 pounds and this thing outside has me feeling like an infant to give a better feel to the hole situation.

fter it urinated I was really freaking out. 1 maybe 2 steps from having a complete breakdown. I as shaking with tears rolling down my face and my nose running like a child. I'm not ashamed say that either. It was truly the scariest thing I have ever experienced in my life and it was ppening 100 miles from nowhere in the dark with multiple Sasquatches!!! It got quiet after it inated for a short time then it started breathing deeply and heavily when I made another tempt to wake my step dad again. It had a real menacing sound to it and then the other two vatted around the tarp some more. It got quiet again and then from in front of me this time other one or more started throwing rocks and debris at us and it was hitting the tarp from all er from in front of me. It stopped shortly after and got real quiet the two behind my stepdad oved back quite a bit it seemed and they started throwing our firewood around and stomping on e ground and breaking tree limbs.

e commotion almost woke my stepdad up, and had me laying there with my gun pointing back er my head hoping they would just leave already but that wasn't happening. It got quiet again and this time it was quiet for the longest and that made me feel better like maybe they were leaving because I heard a lot of movement trail off into the tree line. As I'm feeling better about the one behind never left and started to urinate again and turned mid way through and finished by urinating behind my head on the tarp and followed that up with a low grumbled growl that I felt reverberate through my body and shook the tarp.

That was the final straw and I lost it. I had a small 3 foot long rake we used in camp in with me in case it rained and I had to push the water up off the tarp. I threw it at my stepdad and started screaming for him to wake up. The rake had an aluminum handle that hit the metal sided cot and my stepdad's arm then bounced and hit the trailer railing just making a hell of a noise. The one behind me backed off and made some weird noise I can't describe. My stepdad finally woke up and was pretty upset I hit him with a rake and woke him up. During that time, the ones out in front of me started throwing things again at the tarp. I'm yelling, telling him what's going on and that we're surrounded by these things. He grabs his gun and flash light half groggy and starts climbing over me to go out and investigate. I told him he's crazy and followed because I felt going alone was probably suicide.

We climb out and there's tracks everywhere, good tracks, bad tracks, tracks with claws coming off the toes. Our firewood is everywhere, and a big chunk was torn off a tree from approximately 11 feet up. To my left is the truck and the thickest brush and trees and I can hear one moving in there. The ones out in front that were throwing rocks started throwing rocks at us and the two that were behind my stepdad had come back up behind the trailer and started shaking it. I'm expressing to my stepdad that I no longer want to be there anymore. He simply replied with, get in the truck!

Ve got in the truck and during that the thick brush 5 yards from the truck started shaking

iolently and so did a large mature tree. We got in the truck and started to leave. We couldn't

ave fast because if was incredibly muddy. We never saw one on the way out. We were both

lent and watching out for them on the way out and when we hit the pavement finally, I just shut

own with my gun between my legs pointed at the floor in a complete state of shock. I remember

y stepdad couldn't believe what little he saw and experienced but he wasn't freaking out like I

as. He experienced 5 minutes maybe of what went on and I endured an hour and a half. When

e turned the truck on I felt like it had been 3 or 4 hours this was going on and the clock read

):35pm. I couldn't believe it. He tried getting my gun from me because I guess I looked really

istable but he wasn't getting it he had to settle for me un-chambering the round.

e didn't know what to do after that but we needed to go to the town of XXXXXXXXXX the

xt morning so we drove there, which was 28 miles north of where we were so I gradually

gained my composure and got a really crappy few hours of sleep in the truck in a parking in

XXXXXXXXX.

orning came. We hit the store then needed to head back to the camp we had left the night

fore. I fully expected to find everything in shambles and ripped up to some degree, but when

e arrived, it looked as if we had never left minus the fire wood being all thrown around.

e started packing up camp because we sure as hell were not going to stay there anymore. We

d to get the hitch off the side by side to tow the trailer out with the truck but it was cemented in

om all the mud so I had to beat this thing out with a small sledge hammer. It made a hell of a

ise up the canyon so if anything was around it was going to know we were there. I have to add

at it rained rather hard after we left the night before and all tracks had been destroyed to the point of not being able to photograph them and have them be useful at all so that's why there is no track photos.

It was 10-15 minutes after I got the hitch out we finished loading up. I was loading the last ice chest onto the trailer turned around to talk to my step dad who was talking to me and noticed some movement at my upper right, right at 35 yards away on the low ridgeline on the north side of camp. I turn my head a little more and sure enough I'm staring at a Sasquatch who is staring straight back at me. It was 8:30am against a cloudless piercing blue sky. It had to of wanted us to see it. It didn't appear to be trying to hide and had purposely sky lined itself. Something that everything in the animal kingdom knows you don't do. That's without a doubt the easiest way to get yourself spotted, skyline yourself and move.

It lasted about 4 seconds and then ran up hill into the ravine. This thing was fast and always stayed really low to the ground. It had a burnt auburn, cinnamon colored hair that covered everything I saw on it which was from mid torso on up. It had thinner looking hair on the chest and thicker on the arms. I would have to guess the length at 4 maybe 5 inches. The face had a wide smashed down looking nose with piercing dark eyes that looked recessed back into the head more than you or me. The exposed skin on the face was lighter colored than the hair with slightly darker buckskin kind of coloration. It didn't have a mustache and had a low wide mouth and jaw line that seemed very robust with a slight conical shaped head that seemed to come directly out of the shoulders with no visible neck. It had very wide shoulders that were probably two or more of me with very large pectoral muscles. This was definitely a male.

I can't really give a good height estimate because it seemed to be squatted down throughout the sighting and even when it left I felt it was severely crouched or running on all fours. 7-8 feet or

gger maybe I really am not sure. I did see a hand when it turned to leave. It swung its left arm
above the ridgeline and you could clearly see a five fingered hand that was quite large. I was
e only one to see this as my stepdad had his back turned and only turned quick enough to see
e sagebrush moving that it had hit when it ran. We promptly got in the truck and left after that
appened.

e left and headed for a forest service campground that was about 8-10 miles away. We figured
e had obviously setup camp in an area that seemed to be important to these creatures so we
ent for something that had been a designated campground for 10's of years already hoping they
ould stay away. It didn't work but they didn't get that angry attitude they had before. There was
few exceptions but they were way more docile with us in our new spot. I don't remember the
der in how the nights played out because we spent 10 total nights there and I wasn't
cumenting the events but I can give you what happened when they came around.

e first night was quiet but I couldn't sleep for obvious reasons. The night of the 8th I was
eling a lot better about the whole situation as our buddy Mike was joining us for the next 7
ys and he has been hunting this particular area for the last 42 years and knows the area like the
ck of his hand. Having 3 guys in camp was just a good confidence booster because Mike was a
ht sleeper like myself, and there was one more gun in the mix now. Mike arrived just before
ndown on Friday the 8th. We got him all setup in camp ate some dinner and filled Mike in on
at happened the night of the 6th and morning of the 7th. He thought we were pulling his leg
t quickly realized the seriousness of what we were saying as we were not joking and very
amant about what we were saying. Mike is one of the few people I told of my first encounter
he thought we were joking about that because who does this crap happen to, twice?

Anyway, my stepdad went to bed and me and Mike sat by the fire talking about the other events. After a while we started hearing noises a little ways off and let the fire burn out because the moon was almost full and you could see a thousand times better without the fire. Anyone who has spent time out under a full moon with no canopy overhead knows how bright it can be by a full moon, you can literally read a book by the moon light if you wanted to. The noise kept creeping in closer and got that distinct bipedal signature to it.

Mike couldn't believe what we were hearing. He immediately asked me if I had my gun and I assured him I did and suggested he get his. So we were sitting there and this thing sounded real close, it also sounded like there was just one but I've thought that before and don't believe they travel alone often so we kept listening hard to maybe pickup another one but we never did. So after a while it stopped but we knew it was there because it never seemed to have left. So I turn my flash light on and start doing a sweep around camp. Behind a large tree and bush Mike said he saw a big set of eyes that looked kind of green, so I focused back on that bush and sure enough there was a large set of eyes that appeared to be watching us that looked to have a good or 8 inch spread between them. They even blinked twice before this thing took off running and breaking brush on its way out.

So for the next 3 hours we just sat guard around camp. It really surprised Mike that there was such things happening. He is an older gentleman in his 60's and never experienced anything qu like that. It was another pretty sleepless night. The next morning we went over to the bush we saw the eyes behind and measured up to where were thought they were. It was eight and a half feet up. After that night they all kind of come together into one. There was one night when Mik was still in camp that something came into camp and was walking around and hit one of our ic chests and spun it around. It woke me up a little before 4 am and I was very upset and angry wi ese things by this time so I just started screaming obscenities at it and it woke Mike up at the ame time.

actually climbed out to confront this thing because it seemed to be alone and it ran a ways into e trees and brush. I continued screaming at it while Mike was getting out of his tent and it acked some kind of wood together really fast 3 different times. Mike and me start both reaming at it and it busted a big mature aspen in half and left. The tree was ten inches in ameter when we found it at first light and sounded like a rifle going off. It was loud enough to ake my stepdad who thought we were shooting our guns. The rest of the time all we heard were eavy foot falls and bipedal walking around camp. It also always just seemed to be one of them. was 11 total nights of that kind of stuff and the big encounter at the beginning.

---

hose are just some of the encounters that people have had. Now remember, do not try to pproach a Big Foot. Big Foots are creatures. They can be dangerous. It is better really in my pinion to treat them as if they are dangerous. Do not try to think you are expert after this book. ou are not. This book is just to give you understanding. Now some will say this book is lies. hat is fine. The point of all is there is a creature out there that is known is the Big Foot. This eature is huge. We know nothing really about them. We only know that they are there. There e many different types and names they go by. The one thing in common with everyone is we not know if they are dangerous or not. I would not want to find out if you ask me.

eferences

Sottile, L. (2016, July 5). The man who created Bigfoot. Retrieved July 10, 2016, from tp://www.outsideonline.com/2095096/man-who-created-bigfoot

2.   BFRO. (2016). The Bigfoot-Giganto theory. Retrieved July 10, 2016, from

http://www.bfro.net/REF/THEORIES/MJM/whatrtha.asp

3.   LeClaire, L. (2014, April 4). 10 Bigfoot-Type Cryptids you may not know about.

Retrieved July 10, 2016, from Weird Stuff, http://listverse.com/2014/04/04/10-bigfoot-type-

cryptids-you-may-not-know-about/

4.   Bigfoot encounters. Retrieved July 10, 2016, from http://www.bigfootencounters.com

5.   Research, S. T. B., & profile, V. my complete. (2015, May 20). Nevada Sasquatch.

Retrieved July 10, 2016, from http://nevadasasquatch.blogspot.com/2015/05/bigfoot-hunters

encounter-agressive.html